The Trouble with Palm Trees

Iris Berry

Punk ★ Hostage ★ Press

The Trouble with Palm Trees

Copyright © Iris Berry 2021
An imprint of Punk Hostage Press
ISBN: 978-1-940213-16-3

All rights reserved. Printed in the United States of America. No part of this text may be used or reproduced in any manner whatsoever without written permission from the author or publisher except in the case of brief quotations embodied in critical articles and reviews. For information address. Punk Hostage Press, Hollywood, California.

Cover Photo
Iris Berry

Illustrations
Scott Aicher

Special Thank Yous to:
A Razor, Joe Donnelly,
Amanda "Mandy" Toland,
Johnny Indovina,
Judy Horsefield, and Lola.

Punk Hostage Press

Hollywood, California
www.punkhostagepress.com

For Vicky Hamilton

The Trouble with Palm Trees

Poems by Iris Berry

Contents

The Trouble with Palm Trees

Christmas in Van Nuys
at Ralph's Market at Midnight

The King of the Forbes Avenue
(For Boris the cat rip)

Paper Hearts

What Makes Eddie Run
(For Eddie Little rip)

Feral Like Me
(For Lola the cat)

My Hollywood Boulevard

Shooting for the Stars in Kevlar

Misguided Hearts

Rehab Suitcase

The Ghosts of Punk Rock Past

As Good as it Gets

*The heat
has finally broke
we sit in our backyard
at midnight
surrounded by
fruit trees
cactus and
rose bushes
the coyotes howl
we listen
and they let us…*

The Trouble with Palm Trees

Part #1

Palm trees
standing gorgeous
erect and regal
they call to me
they whisper things
to each other
they glisten in the hot
California sun
they promise
many things
to many people
fame
fortune
love
sweet summer romance…
somehow
all I ever got from them
is they're nice
to look at
and they've never
let me down.

The Trouble with Palm Trees

Part #2

The problem
with palm trees is
there's nothing
practical about them
they offer no shade
in the summer
and no warmth
in the winter
they just
look good
how perfect
for California.

Christmas in Van Nuys at Ralph's Market at Midnight

The lights are cruel
at Ralph's Market
in Van Nuys at midnight.
Apparently, it's Christmas
according to the aisles
at Ralph's Market.
But if I had to guess
by the customers
I'd say it was Halloween.
It's desperate here
in Ralph's
at midnight
and the lights don't help.
Florescent lights
are never good
for the complexion.

There's a young
homeless couple
walking the aisles
buying food
and looking happy
at least they're in a relationship
I think to myself.

Freshly home
from a trip
to *The Big Apple*
I went with my boyfriend
and came home single.

*We had to go
3,000 miles to break up?*

It happened
in bed
in the dark
at 3 in the morning
in a dingy
Times Square
hotel room
It was epic
and when
that plane landed
20 hours later
on California soil
I clicked my heels
and quietly chanted

*there's no place like home
there's no place like home
there's no place like home.*

And now I am home
in my neighborhood Ralph's Market
feeling like I don't belong.

The thing about California
with its constant sunshine
the only way to tell the seasons
is by what's selling on the shelves
at the Supermarkets.

I have a thing for the Supermarket
it's a form of meditation

nothing in here
reminds me
of *my* life

I can do this...
I'm a spiritual giant
in the frozen food section
I'm Gandhi
in the Greeting Card section
and I'm Mother Teresa
in the check-out line
forgiving all
the tabloid sinners
and connecting
with something
greater than all of this.

"Credit or debit?
Paper or plastic?"

"Peace, please…"
I'd like
to give
it a chance
after all
it is
the Holidays.

The King of the Forbes Avenue

(*For Boris the cat rip*)

The day you
kicked the bucket
every living thing
on Forbes Avenue
that was smaller
and couldn't
outrun you
threw a celebration
but not me
I threw a fit.

The neighbor
who brought
you home
in a hefty bag
never wants
to see me again
and as for the guy
who hit you
well
it wasn't his fault
you heard me calling you
and darted straight out
of that field
and you didn't look
you never looked
when I called you
never
you just came home
like the loyal cat

that you were
you came home
for the last time.

And when that car
screeched on its brakes
and hit you
every gopher
on the block
did the can-can
every rat,
mouse and squirrel
threw confetti
and passed out cigars
and in French accents
they chanted
"Viva Le Forbes"
at a thunderous roar.

Every crow was smiling
and every sparrow
was doing the two-step
all in honor of your passing
at the news of your death
at the coming of your going.

Yes, you made
quite an impression
and left your legacy behind
you were definitely
the King of my jungle
you were good
and I'm sorry your stay
on this earth

was a short one
it was brief
but it sure
meant a lot
to me…

Paper Hearts

Sometimes
I picture
a different
kind of life
for us.
Free and simple
where dreams
are still in the lead
and financial fear
isn't winning.
The fear of mortality
hasn't set in
and we're in a setting
in the middle of nowhere
that takes on
a kind of 1970s
noir sensibility
and values.
A time before
we hadn't hurt
or unintentionally
betrayed each other
and broke promises
because someone else
had a better deal
that lasts only as long
as 4 am conversations do,
as we were just trying
to figure it all out.
A time before
we had no past

and our future
was still bright
seamless and
filled with hope.

But fear of intimacy
comes in so many
different forms
and so does
fear of rejection
throw in some
unintentional neglect
and you have
the perfect destination
where love
goes to die.

It's a brutal tragedy
with a cliché ending
I do hope you find
whatever it is
you're looking for
lost out there
in your own private
John Huston film.
And this time
with a much
happier ending.

What Makes Eddie Run

(For Eddie Little rip.)

I see you sitting
sitting in the glow
of your computer
burnt spoon and needle
at one side
and a loaded gun
at your other.

There's only one bullet
in the chamber
and it's reserved for you
you're attempting to write
the next great American novel
and I believe you will
providing you don't kill yourself
before it's finished.

It's a race
isn't it?
Your conscience
and your ego
are at a dead heat
while your phone
is ringing off the hook
with calls from your agent
and London and New York
all wanting to buy the movie rights.

You were the first guy
to ever buy me diamonds

I'm just wondering
where you got the money;
was it an insurance scam?
Phony credit cards?
Or your usual
selling phony stocks
to old people
for their life savings?

Well, all I can say is
it's only a matter of time
for you sweetheart
but if it's true
that nice guys and gals
finish last
than you can bet
I'll be sitting
in the last seat
in the last row
of the house
that I more than likely
bought at 100% mark-up
trapped between
a noisy bathroom
and a rank alleyway.

But at least
while I'm sitting
on the lap of time
checking my watch
I know you'll be
mixing another shot
of liquid comfort
while running

from that god awful mirror
called your conscience.

There aren't enough opiates
in the city of L.A.
to make that reflection go away
but I know you
you're not a quitter
you'll die trying.

Feral Like Me
(For Lola the cat)

I think about you
and how much
we're alike
both left for dead
on streets,
too angry
and brutal
with people
that have love
on their lips
and blood lust
in their eyes
hearts
souls
and groins
as they dangle
the carrot
and say
here kitty, kitty.

I look at you
and think
how much
we're alike
both left for dead
on streets littered
with venom
vacant of empathy
and painted
with empty promises
at the intersections

of *Fuck You*
and *Fuck Me*.
Intersections
that devour souls
at a mere whisper
and the hearsay
of love
vulnerability
honesty
and the scent
of kindness.

I look at you
and think
how much
we're alike
we were both
left for dead
by the very ones
that gave us life.

I know
I saved you
as you were being
swallowed
by a quicksand
of leaves
an old tire
a carburetor
and houses
foreclosed
out there
in the avenues
and the streets

where souls
go to die
and the last things
that come
the closest
to touching
their unwanted bodies
are chalk
and tape
for protection
that came
just a little too late.

I look at you
as you
lay beside me
I feel warm
knowing
I saved you
and you
saved me.

I put my hand out
to touch your face
and you bite me
and then you lick
as if to apologize
for your nature
your instinct
and I let you
as I know
you only
do it
because

you're feral
like me
and I love you for it
all the more...

My Hollywood Boulevard

All through the 1980s
it was breakfast at the Rexall Fountain
on Hollywood Boulevard and Highland Avenue,
or Snow White's coffee shop,
where eating there
felt like some sort of
Disney ride on acid
with all the boulevard mutants,
much more effective
than any ride
I'd gone on at Disneyland.
There was the Las Palmas Bookstand
and Miceli's Restaurant
and of course Red's Baroque Books,
with the finest and complete
Bukowski collection around.
It didn't get any better than Red's.
There was Hollywood Book & Poster
for all your Horror and B-Movie needs,
for the real memorabilia jones.
There was Musso & Franks,
and Jojo down at Book City
with every paperback and hardback
classic known to man.
Grecco's with all the
heavy-metal-white-trash runaways
and a slice of MTV
with your pizza.
And across the street
Frederick's Of Hollywood
looking like a giant Wurlitzer,

always pumping out
that slow bump 'n' grind,
right there in the middle of it all,
and to this day
the best shoes in all of Hollywood.
There was J.J. Newberry's
and the magic shop.
Johnny's Steak House
for that $3.95 steak dinner,
and it was good.
Hooray For Hollywood
for cheap rock 'n' roll T-shirts,
three for 10 dollars.
And of course Playmates of Hollywood,
which started out
as a children's store
and grew up with its customers,
from toddler to stripper.
Then there were the bars;
The Zero One After-Hours
right above Playmates
when David Lee Roth owned it.
The Frolic Room #2,
Boardner's,
The Gaslight,
The Firefly,
the original Frolic Room,
The Cathay de Grande,
home of fine punk rock.
The Vine Bar & Grill
for Blues and Jazz,
and last but not least
Raji's where you could see
Screamin' Jay Hawkins

the Vandals and TSOL
all in one night.
And then on the outskirts
of Hollywood Boulevard
were all the places I lived;
The Cliffwood Manor,
Disgraceland,
The Havenhurst,
and The Fontenoy,
surrounded by churches, schools,
auto mechanic places
and cheap dirt-bag, dope fiend motels,
with the letters always
burned out in the signs,
the kind of places
that only look good
in the movies
and only sound interesting
in a Tom Waits song.
Like The Mark Twain,
The Saint James,
The Saint Moritz
and The Sunset 8.
Yes, Hollywood in the 80's
was a great time.
it was before Crack and AIDS,
it was the coming and going
of Ronald Reagan
and before all the real damage
he did as President hit,
before homeless was normal.
Now I look at Hollywood Boulevard
and it's just like a former lover
grown old and alcoholic,

an old lover that never took care of itself.
My two favorite times
to catch Hollywood Boulevard
used to be at dusk and at dawn.
At dusk when the sun was barely out
but all the neon was on,
and in the morning
before pedestrians.
Raymond Chandler put it best
when he said, "Hollywood Boulevard
at sun-up is like an aging hooker
without her make-up on."
Now it's like that
around the clock and worse.
And when the L.A. riots hit
and Hollywood was burning,
I thought, "Oh no, not my Hollywood Boulevard."
But it's not my Hollywood anymore,
now it belongs to the gangs,
the mutant homeless,
the corporate conglomerates
and the tourists.
The new Americana,
God bless them all.
No, it's not my Hollywood anymore,
but Hollywood in the 80s
was a great time,
it was my Paris in the 20s,
and yes, a good time
was had by all.

Shooting for the Stars in Kevlar

we run
from hot summer days
and broken air conditioners

we run
to chilled movie theatres
make out like teenagers
who've never had sex
never been kissed

by tender mouths
and never cradled
in the arms
of an unconditional love

we make our own movies
back in the back of the theatre
laughing like there's no yesterday
yesterdays that begged us to stay
and tried to kill us
in our sleep
then chased us
in our waking hours
begging for salvation
and a hall pass

we are the bright spots in the road
found in dark alleys

a pair of lives
lived hard
treated hard
and discarded harder
and as we hit
the pavement
skipping
we forgot
that we were only playing
hopscotch
to the tune of songs
lead by a symphony
of sirens and howling dogs

can we believe

that we can believe in love?
after we have let so many
put their unloving hands
around our hearts
souls and throats

x-friends
x-loves
x-cons
x-drug habits
x-drug dealers
still trying to strike a better deal
with empty promises
empty pockets
and empty souls

leaving
open wounds
like bullets holes
as the winds
blow through them
hollow and scarred
and that sometimes
most often
are unhealable

a catalog
of catastrophic events
shaped our lives
and sculpted us
into who we are.

it doesn't always mean
that who we are

can carry us
into who we want to be…

but that doesn't mean we'll stop trying

as we dry our eyes
while no one's looking
in dark theaters
waiting for
 the next movie
to start…

Misguided Hearts

This is an open letter
an open love-letter
to no one
and to everyone
everyone I've ever been with
or wanted to be with
or will be with in the future
I'm here to say
I've had it all wrong
nothing was your fault
it was all me
not you
I know that tired old line…
but it's true
I picked you
expected you to deliver
things we never discussed
and expected you to be psychic
in the name of love
I didn't take into mind
that we were not
right for each other
or that our love
was not written in the stars
and our karma
didn't even go together
like some accidental god
I was a cupid imposter
a double agent
in the house of love
attempting to shape fate

and bend time
and I'm just so sorry
from the bottom
of my misguided heart

and whatever you do
please don't forgive me
trust me
it'll be easier this way…

Rehab Suitcase

They all
look the same
always packed
in a hurry
and usually filled
with nothing useful…

Mine had:
2 iPhones
4 burner phones
a worn-down black eye pencil
that had seen better days
and pens from places like
Caesar's Palace,
the Barbary Coast Casino,
and Bun Boy's
the Largest Thermometer in The World,
all of them out of ink.
Used make-up
that would never get used
plastic CVS bags filled with
lighters that didn't work,
phone numbers on napkins
that would never get called
stray and orphaned socks
that belonged to no other sock
Blonde Maybelline eyebrow pencils
still in the packet
purchased from some other decade
and Target bags filled with
brand new clothes

that had no scent
of 4 am cigarette smoke
after-hour bar booze
or the memory
of anything awful at all
except *this* rehab suitcase
packed with the frenetic energy
of a person trying to escape.

Rehab Suitcases
they all look the same
Destination:

anywhere but here…

The Ghosts of Punk Rock Past

The first time we met
was on a Saturday night in 1978 or '79.
He was running down Sunset Boulevard
with about
five other people
they were all covered in peanut butter.

He stopped right in front of me
and sweetly said,
"We're smearing peanut butter
all over ourselves,
you wanna do it with us?"

My friends were horrified
and pulled me away.
I was intrigued.

About a year later
we were in his apartment
on Cherimoya and Franklin
which was literally
in the shadow
of the Hollywood Sign.
There was about 10 kittens
running around
and bouncing off the walls,
it was a flying cat circus.

He liked to say my name backwards,
"Hey, Siri! Give me your arm?"
and before I knew it
he grabbed my wrist
and just as his lit cigarette
was about to hit my skin
one of the kittens
flew into us
and knocked it
out of his hands.

The last time
I saw him
was at Oki Dog
It was about 2:30
in the morning
he was walking around
saying goodbye
to people
one by one...
and the next day
just like that
he was gone.

Since then
there's been
so many others
and I think about it
these encounters
brief and fleeting
and otherwise.
These bonds
surreal and otherworldly
in life as in death.
These chance meetings.
And I don't know
what any of it means
I'm just glad
we met
along the way…

As Good as it Gets

In the past two years
I've learned
that just because
you're loyal,
honest
and devoted
does not mean
it will
be reciprocated.
that sometimes,
sadly, no good deed
goes unpunished
and most movies
do not resemble
real life
especially the ones
with the big budgets
and what my grandmothers
told me about men
is true.

I've also learned
that no matter
how much
you know
and love somebody
they can still
have secrets
that could
break your heart
and possibly kill you.

Don't rely
on fortune cookies
but never let
a good wishbone
go to waste
and that nothing is personal
and everything is personal
no one is perfect
especially me
and the more
mistakes I make
the more human and nice
I am towards you
and the more powerful I think I am
the more danger
I am in

I've learned
that everyone dies
some quickly
some slowly
so it's best
to live the life
you really want
it's taken me forever
to realize
that I still
haven't grown-up
and that somehow
I still have the fantasy
that as long as I am a good person
life will get better.
But what I've really learned is

the clock is tick-tick ticking
and maybe
I should do my best
to leave this place
with a smile on my face
and love in my heart
for you
and for me
and maybe
that's as good as it gets

and if that's the case
I will consider
myself
lucky…

The End

Iris Berry is a native Angelino and one of the true and original progenitors of the L.A. punk scene. She is the author of several books including *Two Blocks East of Vine, The Daughters of Bastards, The Underground Guide to Los Angeles* and *All That Shines Under the Hollywood Sign*. Internationally known, her wit and often dark, factual accuracy and empathy for her subjects has brought her critical acclaim as well as a huge fan base. She writes her experiences with grace and deadly precision. Her lullaby-and bedtime-story voice is like a haunting tour of Los Angeles that lingers like one of the city's unsolved murders.

Berry has appeared in numerous films, TV commercials, documentaries, and iconic rock videos. In the 1980s she was a singer for the punk band the Lame Flames. Later Berry co-founded and toured extensively with her band The Ringling Sisters, who recorded with legendary producer Lou Adler (A&M Records). Berry also sang and wrote songs and recorded with the Dickies, the Flesh Eaters and Pink Sabbath. **She's received two certificates of merit from the city of Los Angeles for her contribution as a Los Angeles writer/historian and for her extensive charity work. From 2010-2014 she was on the Board of Directors for Beyond Baroque Literary/Arts Center. Iris is the co-founder, editor and publisher for her imprint PUNK HOSTAGE PRESS** where continues to champion for original voices.

About The Illustrator

Scott Aicher's love for art began at the early age of five when he won 3 blue ribbons after his mother entered his paintings in a local art show. Largely a self-taught artist, he has had many years of experience as a professional artist starting in humble print shops, then later advancing to illustration for entertainment, record and surf companies. Scott's work can be seen on various flyers and record covers for: Bad Religion, Pennywise, Firehose, Chemical People, Jeff Dahl, Rikk Agnew, TSOL, the Angry Samoans, Chicano Batman, Mike Watt, Toys That Kill, Rolling Blackouts, Love Canal, Blood on the Saddle, Left Insane and Nip Drivers to name a few. Along with illustrating two books by TSOL front man Jack Grisham, *Untamed* and *Code Blue* (Punk Hostage Press). And Iris Berry's *All That Shines Under the Hollywood Sign* and *The Trouble with Palm Trees* (Punk Hostage Press).

    Growing up in Southern California provided much of the outlandish cartoon style that breathes throughout his work. Often playful with a bright bold color pallet his work falls mainly in the Pop Surreal or Kustom Culture genres. He collects Toys, Vinyl Records, Comics, Art Books and Guitars. He and his family moved to Texas. They love the open space and wildlife there and especially the southern hospitality. It's rough finding a good Pizza, but he's enjoying the pimento cheese sandwiches.

More Books on Punk Hostage Press

Danny Baker
    Fractured - 2012

A Razor
    Better Than a Gun in A Knife Fight - 2012
    Drawn Blood: Collected Works
    From D.B.P.LTD., 1985-1995 - 2012
    Beaten Up Beaten Down - 2012
    Small Catastrophes in A Big World - 2012
    Half- Century Status - 2013
    Days of Xmas Poems - 2014
    Puro Purismo - 2021

Iris Berry
    The Daughters of Bastards - 2012
    All That Shines Under the Hollywood Sign – 2019
    The Trouble with Palm Trees - 2021

C.V. Auchterlonie
    Impress - 2012

Yvonne De la Vega
    Tomorrow, Yvonne - Poetry & Prose for Suicidal Egoists - 2012

Carolyn Srygley- Moore
    Miracles Of the Blog: A Series - 2012

Rich Ferguson
    8th & Agony -2012

Jack Grisham
    Untamed -2013
    Code Blue: A Love Story ~ 2014
    Pulse of the World. Arthur Chance, Punk Rock Detective - 2021

Dennis Cruz
    Moth Wing Tea - 2013
    The Beast Is We - 2018

Frank Reardon
    Blood Music - 2013

Pleasant Gehman
    Showgirl Confidential – 2013
    Rock 'n' Roll Witch – A Memoir of Sex Magick, Drugs and Rock 'n' Roll - 2022

Hollie Hardy
    How To Take a Bullet and Other Survival Poems – 2014

Joel Landmine
    Yeah, Well... – 2014
    Things Change - 2021

More Books on Punk Hostage Press

A.D. Winans
    Dead Lions – 2014
S.A. Griffin
    Dreams Gone Mad with Hope - 2014
SB Stokes
    History Of Broken Love Things – 2014
Nadia Bruce- Rawlings
    Scars - 2014
    Driving in The Rain - 2020
Lee Quarnstrom
    WHEN I WAS A DYNAMITER, Or, how a Nice Catholic Boy Became a Merry Prankster, a Pornographer, and a Bridegroom Seven Times - 2014
Alexandra Naughton
    I Will Always Be Your Whore/Love Songs for Billy Corgan - 2014
    You Could Never Objectify Me More Than I've Already Objectified Myself -2015
Michele McDannold
    Stealing The Midnight from A Handful of Days – 2014
Maisha Z Johnson
    No Parachutes to Carry Me Home - 2015
Michael Marcus
    #1 Son and Other Stories - 2017
Danny Garcia
    LOOKING FOR JOHNNY, The Legend of Johnny Thunders - 2018
William S. Hayes
    Burden of Concrete - 2020
Todd Moore
    Dillinger's Thompson - 2020
Dan Denton
    $100-A-Week Motel - 2021
Jack Henry
    Driving W/ Crazy, living with madness – 2021
Joe Donnelly
    So Cal, Dispatches From the End of the World - 2022
Patrick O'Neil
    Anarchy at the Circle K – On the Road with Dead Kennedys, TSOL, Flipper, Subhumans… and Heroin – 2022

www.ingramcontent.com/pod-product-compliance
Lightning Source LLC
Chambersburg PA
CBHW032103040426
42449CB00007B/1168